THE ROAD
TO FINDING
YOURSELF

by Melissa Cohen

Table of Contents

PREFACE

A few years ago, I was going through some difficult problems and getting very overwhelmed. According to people I spoke with, my feelings of anxiety, fear, and of being overwhelmed were perfectly justified, considering my circumstances at the time. In fact, people told me that it's perfectly normal for the house and the kids to get a little out of control, and for you and your husband to have fights. Because I bought those words, all of their "prophecies" slowly started to come true in my life. Finally, I got to a point where I could not see any way out of these feelings. I thought that, because of my circumstances and problems, I was stuck with them. Needless to say, my life started looking more and more gloomy. I thought that maybe I could find a solution by seeing a therapist. The problem was that she was also caught up in my circumstances, and so she tried to give me her techniques and her good ideas on how to handle things better. As with all therapists, she was sincerely doing exactly what she was trained to do. Because of my thoughts, emotions, and circumstances, she thought of me as someone broken who needed to be fixed. They were trying to fix me, or at least help me fix myself, and unfortunately that approach was not working.

One day a friend of mine called me and suggested that she and I learn this new approach called 'Innate Health' or 'The Three Principles'. I have to say that I was not very enthusiastic. In fact, I told her to leave me alone, that it was not for me. I had had enough of therapy. She kept insisting. She said that this was not therapy as I understood it, and that I should please try it with her. Eventually (thank G-d) I agreed.

Within a very short time of starting to learn these principles, the experience of my life entirely changed. Even though the same circumstances or problems were still there, my experience of these problems was different. I began to understand that I was not feeling these emotions because of my circumstances. *In fact my circumstances had nothing to do with what I was feeling at all.* Understanding this and believing it gave me my life back. Now, I was no longer trapped waiting for circumstances to change in order to be happy. I no longer had to wait for things to be different for my kids to behave better or my husband to be less stressed.

As I started understanding the role thought plays in my life, I started to feel better. And as I started to feel better, my inner wisdom and common sense started to resurface. Problems that looked unsolvable suddenly became solvable: a marriage that seemed almost lost was saved, and difficult kids were suddenly much easier and more lovable. Yet nothing had changed except my relationship to my thinking.

The major difference between this approach and modern therapy is very simple. We don't believe people need to be 'fixed'. We believe that people are equipped from birth to resolve and deal with the problems that come to them. Human beings think there is something wrong, or that life is hopeless because the set of circumstances they were given is too hard, or not something they can deal with. Or they think something is wrong with them because something bad has happened to them, or because they have feelings of fear and anxiety in the first place. Unfortunately, modern therapists usually believe that as well, and thus reinforce those beliefs in their clients, and a vicious cycle ensues. When we realize that this is not true, we take back control of our lives. We define who we are, not with some label or through our circumstances, but who we are essentially. When we do that, the possibilities are limitless.

I started teaching these principles more or less by accident a few years ago. A friend of mine was having a really horrible time, much worse than mine ever was. She was feeling completely devastated, scared and hopeless. The only way I could think of to help her was to teach her this approach. Within a very short time, she changed. She was able to smile, laugh and feel hopeful again. She was able to let go of her anger and fear. Although her circumstances are still very difficult, her peace of mind has become remarkable. You would never know from her attitude that she has any difficult circumstances at all in her life. After I saw the changes in both myself and someone else, I started to teach more people. I have taught people that have been in therapy for years and after a four-day intensive with some follow up, they are different people. Every one of my clients has asked me how I am accomplishing what years of therapy have not. I tell them that I am only inviting them to see something that they have not seen before. I am inviting them to take a look at who they really are, and to stop looking at who they *think* they are. I am inviting them to see that their emotions start from within and project outward. We do not start from outside of ourselves and project inward. It is an inside out world not and outside in world.

I have been learning these principles for over six years, and I have been sharing these principles with clients and friends for over four years. I give four-day intensives, seminars, and teleconferences. I deal with marital issues, parenting, addictions, mental health issues, anxiety, and stress. I have also done some teaching for business. My practice is based out of Brooklyn, New York.

Any person with any and every kind of problem, from addictions to depression, to mental illness, chemical imbalance, anxiety fear, stress, or someone that just wants a better experience of life can benefit from learning this approach. Even business owners that want to grow their business can benefit from learning these principles.

INTRODUCTION

I have always had the feeling that soon I will find the answers I have been looking for, but somehow those answers were always just beyond my reach. No matter how many books on psychology that I read and learned, what I was looking for was always just ahead of me, almost in my grasp, but not quite there.

I am happy to say that I have finally found what I have been searching for. I call it 'the missing link'. This information is what ties together all of my learning and exploring of myself and of G-d. This understanding has affected my life in every way. I am a better wife, mother, daughter, and friend. Most of all, I am a better person. What I have found is my psychological health, or in plain English, peace of mind. I don't want to sound like I never had peace of mind before, because that is not true. There have been times when I have felt happy and peaceful, but there have been many times when I did not. I could never hold on to the happy, peaceful feeling; it seemed to come when it wanted and would leave just as mysteriously. What I was searching for was how to get that feeling to stay.

When I say I found peace of mind, I don't mean either that I now walk around all day calm and peaceful (although I find that I do that a lot more than I ever did before). I mean that I have found a place inside where my inner wisdom and peace, strength and compassion, and inner joy live. I have found that the keys to peace of mind and happiness are not in outside circumstances, but within. The more I live from that inner place, the more things seem to make sense and the less effort I have to make.

The benefit of learning this approach is that after we have internalized it, we get to live it. There is no comparison between the life we had before and the life we have after. It is the difference between existing and feeling really alive.

Before learning about these principles, I used to take life way too seriously. I was always scared, anxious and stressed. I thought that many things were problems I had to solve. I had to figure things out and always be one step ahead of the game. For example, if I would start to work on a project, I would constantly think of every problem that might come up and how to deal with it from a hundred different angles in case it did happen. I would constantly be on the lookout for what might go wrong. If a problem occurred that I hadn't thought of, I would go into a panic and try to figure out how to solve it or head it off. If things didn't work out the way I felt they should, I would be very critical of myself. As a result, I was constantly living in either the past or the future.

Throughout this whole process, I attributed all my stress and anxiety to the project. When I finished, I would feel better, because after all, it was the project that was making me crazy and stressed.

After I started learning about the principles, I started seeing for myself that I could work on a project and be calmer while doing so, based on the thoughts I was paying attention to. I was able to solve problems more easily and with more common sense and inner wisdom than I ever did before. Instead of living in anticipation of a problem, I chose to live in the moment – where there was no problem – and solve or work on the resolution to a problem only when and if it came up. That alone took almost all the stress away. I found that not only was it unhelpful to work on projects in a stressful state, it was actually harmful. I found that I had much more creative ideas while working, and much wiser solutions to the real problems that might come up. Before I learned this approach, I subconsciously thought that stressful thinking was helpful, even necessary.

I learned that the opposite is actually true: stressful thinking is not necessary and could actually ruin the project.

What I came to realize was that in my mind, everything was a project, from parenting to marriage, to business, to weight loss, to friendships, but when I would stay in the present moment, all of these things seem to work.

In these chapters, we are going to explore the journey we can all take to get to that place of health and wholeness and contentment that is found within every human being. Enjoy it; I do.

CHAPTER 1

Principles

First, we need to talk about principles. A principle is an underlying fact of how nature works. The principle of gravity says that what goes up must come down. Does anything change if I don't believe in the principle of gravity? Gravity doesn't care. I know this because no matter how many times I throw an apple in the air, it falls back to earth. A principle has nothing to do with what we believe. Whether or not we believe in the principle, or are even aware of it, it still exists.

How does it help us to know about principles?

Let's go back to the example of gravity. Even though Newton had discovered this principle, we realized that human beings could not fly. But we also knew that certain species of animals could fly. It wasn't until we understood the principles of aerodynamics that we were able to work within those principles and make them work for us to counter the effect of gravity. Then we were able to build airplanes and spaceships. Before we knew enough about gravity and which principles to use to counter its effects, we also tried to build airplanes, but we were never successful. Principles gave us a starting framework from which to build, and the correct starting framework is the key to building anything. If I try to build a building with the incorrect foundation, the building will collapse. Everything we create must start with the correct understanding of the principles at work.

One of the things that I recently discovered was that principles do not only operate outside of ourselves in nature. It should not surprise us to know that human beings were also created with psychological principles. To the extent that we understand these principles, we can build our happiness and have a meaningful life.

What are these psychological principles? There are three: Mind, Thought, and Consciousness. Keep in mind that these principles are just metaphors. We are always looking to see behind the metaphor. We are looking to understand what is before thought, what is before experience. Or in different words, what is the source of thought, or what is the source of our experience? I had always thought it was my circumstances. What I see now is that that is not true.

Mind

Mind is the formless energy behind creation. Mind holds all of what exists in a potential state. When we create something, for example a table or chair, we are taking formless energy and expressing it through a form. Some people refer to Mind as G-d. After all, what is it that makes the heart beat and the blood flow? It is this energy. (Others understand the principle of Mind to be divine in essence, but not the whole of what G-d might be, G-d ultimately being beyond any description.)

Thought

The principle of Thought is the formless energy that takes form through thoughts. Thought is a divine tool that has the potential to allow us to see life as we wish. Where does Thought come from? Thought (and Consciousness as well) comes from the first principle of Mind. Thoughts can come through our higher self and be helpful or true. Or they can come through the ego or the body and be habitual, limiting or unhelpful thoughts. Thoughts we have carried with us our whole lives, thoughts from our parents or our culture, can be misleading and constricting. *Thoughts, freeing or limiting, helpful, or unhelpful, are always the seed of our experience in any circumstance.*

Let me give an example. One person grew up in a family

where, if it was raining, they never went out unless it was an emergency. Another person grew up in a house where they could go out if it was raining. These two different people grew up with very different thoughts about a rainy day. Which one is right? Each one thinks she is right, but the truth is that neither person is right or wrong. Our *thoughts* about the rain (and as we will see, our attachment to these thoughts) are the only things that would cause us to go out in the rain or stay in. The rain itself is neutral; it's just doing what it was created to do. But one person thinks of it – and thus experiences it – as wet and cold and maybe dangerous. The other person doesn't think of it like this; she just experiences it as rain, not something that she needs to stop her life for, and may in fact enjoy.

The important thing for us to understand is that both people can allow the way they think of rain – or the way they think of anything – to change, and thus change their experience.

Let's use another example. Your child comes home in a really bad mood and the first thing she does is say something nasty to you. You could think, 'No child of mine should ever come home and speak that way to me', and feel really angry and end up yelling at her. Or you could feel compassion for her and quietly ask her what's bothering her. Finally, you might feel simply curious about what might have happened in school today that has upset her. The point is that if circumstances dictate how we feel in any given situation then we should not have been able to describe three different reactions to the same situation. What determines these three different reactions is the thinking about the circumstance and, as we shall see, our attachment to that thinking. In the first example, it is your *thought* that she has no right to speak that way that generates a feeling of anger. In the second example, it was your *thought* and your attachment to the thought that something must be bothering her which generates compassion. In the third situation you *thought*, 'I wonder what happened in school', and so you felt curious. All three emotions and reactions were different because the thinking was different in each case.

Consciousness

It is through the principle of Consciousness that what we think becomes experience. But how does this happen? We cannot feel or experience or even perceive any circumstance unless we have a thought about it and unless we attach ourselves to that thought through our consciousness. The way we attach ourselves to a thought is by *believing* the thought. Consciousness begins to take form and express itself first through awareness. Often, we are not even aware that we have had a thought that is defining our experience through our consciousness. The beginning of choosing our experience is the awareness that we have attached ourselves to the thought behind it.

Movies are good metaphors. When a person sees a movie they might laugh or cry or be bored. But nothing real is happening except different lights being projected onto a screen. We have attached ourselves to certain thinking and therefore we cry at a sad movie and laugh at a funny one.

To use an extreme example, if a person is in a coma (G-d forbid), one of the ways a doctor can tell if the person is still alive is if they have brain waves. This fact suggests that even a person in a coma has thoughts. However, if they are not conscious they can't experience their thoughts because they cannot attach themselves to their thoughts without consciousness.

Think about a refrigerator: the refrigerator needs the plug, outlet and compressor in order to work. If I take the plug away, it doesn't work. If I have the plug but take the outlet away, it won't work. And if I leave the outlet and take the compressor away, it also doesn't work. All three components are equally important to having a working refrigerator.

The Principles are no different. Without Mind, there is nothing to give us life and energy at all. If I take Thought away, then I am basically a zombie because I have no way to interpret my circumstances. And if I take Consciousness away, then I am oblivious because I have no way to experience my thoughts. These three principals are active all the time. Through them, each person individually experiences and interprets his or her world. Remember, these principles are active whether we realize it or not. The advantage of realizing them is that life gets a whole lot easier to manage and much more meaningful.

Chapter 2

Our Thoughts Are Not Always Helpful

What makes up a person's thinking? We ask this because, as babies we really live on instinct. A baby cries when it is uncomfortable. It is not thinking "I am hungry now, so let me cry to get my mother's attention." It just knows to cry. As babies, we start out on a very high level of dependence on this energy behind life, but a very low level of awareness of it. If we observe babies or young children, we can see that the majority only cry when they are uncomfortable. They never cry in *anticipation* of being uncomfortable. In other words, babies or young children never say, "Give me extra food now just in case I am hungry later." They instinctively know that when they are hungry or want something, they will try to get it. And even if for some reason they don't get it, they deal with it in the moment, not before. That is why we don't find worried babies or toddlers. At this point they haven't developed any thoughts that would lead to worry. We develop these kinds of thoughts because as children, we watch and learn from our parents, from television and from society. We also have certain life experiences such as traumas or social encounters and start to develop ideas on what those mean. We interpret those situations in certain ways.

A child who was bullied at school might develop a type of thinking that says, "If I weren't so weak, I would not be getting bullied." As a result of the child's attachment or belief in that thought, he might develop more thoughts about how weak he is, which might express themselves as low self-esteem, extreme shyness and fear. However, another child might be bullied at school, and as result, think he will never do that to another person. To the best of his ability, if he sees people getting bullied, he will try to help them. As a result of his attachment to and belief in that thought, he develops more thoughts on how to help people. This in turn could manifest itself into standing up for himself and for others, thus further building his confidence and self-esteem. In these two examples, which experience is true and which is not? In terms of experience, the truth is what you believe it to be. To the first child, his thoughts and thus his experience was true, and to the second child, his thought and thus his experience was also true. What we need to look at is *which thoughts are more helpful.* The thinking of the first child did not lead him to a very happy experience. The thoughts of the second child did lead him to a much more productive and beneficial path.

We mean what we say when we say we create our reality through our thinking. To the extent that we believe or give energy to our thoughts, we will 'follow' them. The circumstance of being bullied is neutral, while what we think about that circumstance is what will determine how we feel about it, which influences the future decisions we may make.

Habitual Thinking

Habitual thinking is thought we have developed from our childhood or from our culture. We believe those thoughts to be true and helpful even if they are not, and we tend to act on them. We need to consider the possibility that thoughts we have now, thoughts we may have had our whole life, may not be helpful. In fact, it is those thoughts that are creating my experience of my life right now. In the bullying example, the little boy continues believing that he is weak because he got bullied. The fact that he got bullied is not causing him to feel weak. He feels weak because he believes the thought that says "I am weak." As soon as he stops taking that thought seriously – the moment he stops giving that thought energy – is the moment he will stop feeling weak, particularly if he energizes a new, positive thought about himself. It doesn't matter if he stops believing that thought five minutes after he had it or fifty years later, his experience of himself and his life will change as soon as he starts realizing how big a part his thinking plays in his life and how small a part all his past "stuff" plays in his life. Habitual thinking consists of habits of thought that we have developed over the years which we think are real, and have a habit of holding onto. As soon as we understand that we do not have to energize and believe every thought we think, we can start to see the same circumstances of our life very differently. This is true regarding our relationships as well. Any person that we have feelings about, those feelings are only there because of what we think of that person. That is why friends can become enemies and enemies can become friends. The only thing that changes in those relationships is our thinking. If we hate someone because they wronged us in some way, and later on we forgive them and develop a friendship with them, the only thing that could have changed is our thinking about what that person did to us. Because in fact the person still wronged us. We simply chose to either stop thinking about it, or to think about the incident in a different way.

What are fear, anxiety, and depression?

To answer this question, I would like to talk about the

principle of "mind", or the formless energy behind life. If we look at the natural world, we see very clearly that some intelligence is behind it. A small apple seed is planted in the ground and a big apple tree emerges. The oceans never pass their sand borders. The sun rises and sets every day. If we asked the smartest scientist in the world to duplicate any of these things, he could not. He may be able to tell us how all these things happen, but he could never make them happen. This same intelligence is behind the human body as well. As far as I can tell, I do not make my own heart beat or my kidneys function, or my legs move for that matter. All these things seem to happen without any help from me. Scientists tell us that everything ultimately needs a power source, which some call "the life force." We know that if this energy stops powering our heart, it would stop and we would die. Every second of every day, this energy enables our heart to pump and give us life. It also gives life to the natural world as well. We can even say that it is only this formless energy that gives life to creation as a whole. Creation in fact is this formless energy in form. This energy shapes itself into forms we call nature and humanity. Thoughts are also this energy in form. Nature and the human body each only refer to this energy for their repair and healing. What happens if I cut my finger? If I leave it alone, it will normally heal itself. But if I pick at it, it will not heal; in fact, it could get worse and get infected.

Wouldn't it make sense that the same applies to the mind?

Our thoughts are flowing all the time. Sometimes they get "cut up," and don't come with a good feeling. If I cut my finger, it also hurts, but because I know it will heal, it doesn't scare me. One of the reasons people get so upset when they have painful thinking is because they aren't sure if those thoughts will go away. But as with the body, if we leave our thoughts alone, our minds will naturally think clearly again. New and better thoughts will naturally flow to us. As with the cut on your finger: if you leave the cut alone it will heal, but if you pick at it, it will get worse. Our minds work the same way. Focusing on an unhelpful thought is the same as picking at the cut. For example, you start feeling down, scared or stressed, Your thinking about that circumstance is what will either keep that low feeling in place or let it go. If we focus on the fact that we feel down, our thoughts could look like this: "Oh no. What's wrong with me; I hate this feeling." Or you could think, "There's that feeling again, no big deal." The first is the same as picking at the cut, and the second is the same as leaving the cut and letting it heal on its own. The less attention we pay to the bad feeling, the faster it will go away.

For this energy to be able to do all this, it must be more intelligent than any human being. As I said, we as human beings, may be able to explain how nature or the body works, but we cannot make them work. This intelligence must be merciful as well because most of us wake up in the morning with everything working pretty well. There has never been a morning when the sun didn't rise. The weather is usually pretty stable, and even when a storm is coming we usually have enough time to prepare. So if this energy (or some would say G-d) goes out of its way to create a beautiful, functional world, does it not make sense for the world to be enjoyable? After all, what do human beings want most of all? Isn't it happiness and peace of mind? But we look around and see so much suffering and so many unhappy people. What has gone wrong?

It seems to me that people look for their happiness and peace of mind from things outside themselves. We look for it in objects or we think that other people could give it to us. But when we look at the rest of creation, we see that well-being and correct functionality relies on this basic energy. It makes sense that our psychological health would also depend on this energy. After all, it would not make sense and would not be very merciful if the things I want in life, peace of mind and happiness, were dependent on other people or objects. What if the other person decides not to do what we want them to, or what if I can't get a certain object? Does that mean I am doomed to unhappiness? If that were true, we would all be victims of other people's moods, and of circumstances. What if that isn't how it is supposed to be, what if just like in nature or for the physical body my peace of mind is also dependent on this fundamental energy? What if happiness comes from an understanding that it's the thoughts I am attached to that will decide my feelings in the moment and not the other person's behavior? When we realize this, we get control of our lives back because we don't need anything or any person to make us happy. I have all the power I need to make myself happy. It really is an inside out world, not an outside in world, which means my feeling start from within me and project outward; they do not start from outside me and project inward.

Much of our thinking comes from trying to figure out how to get something or how to get another person to stop or start doing something. Every advertisement for any product is trying to get you to believe that their product will bring you the happiness you are looking for, but we all know that after we have the item for a while that feeling goes away, because our feelings do not really come from the object. **We are being sold a feeling we already own.** We were born with this sense of wellbeing; it is our birthright. We are given everything we need.

Children know this, which is why they can throw a tantrum in one moment and laugh the next, and why they don't hold grudges. They just let their thoughts flow and live in the moment. Our peace of mind is within us. Our thoughts form the link between our spiritual source and our physical lives. The thoughts we choose to focus on will create our experience of reality in the moment. Remember the definition of thought: it is a divine tool that allows us to view the world any way we wish. That means we can use our gift of thought against ourselves by believing thoughts that will make our experience of the world feel painful. On the other hand I can take responsibility for my own experience and realize that if I am unhappy, I am attached to unhappy thoughts and those thoughts have nothing to do with anyone else. If I want to be happy, it really is quite simple. I only have to understand that I am always feeling my thinking; as the thoughts change so will my experience.

What's so interesting is that the more we listen for and believe the wise helpful thoughts, the more we will be connected to our source and the more those wise helpful thoughts will be available to us, giving our lives meaning and direction. For what are fear, anxiety and depression? Simply, thoughts I believe in and thus live out of. Further, the more of those unhelpful thoughts we believe, the more of those thoughts we will get. It is the same as picking at the cut on our finger. If I just realize they are just thoughts and stop picking at them, they will eventually go away.

When I was pregnant with my fourth child, I was literally terrorizing myself with thoughts about the upcoming birth. The birth before this had not been easy and the fear of this happening again was something I could not stop thinking about. This was before I learned these principles, and I thought I was completely justified in my fears; after all, if it had happened once, it could happen again. After a very long 9 months, the birth went fine but I had literally tortured myself for nine months with my thoughts. This is what I didn't know: While it is true that we **cannot** control the initial thoughts that come into our head, we **can** notice those thoughts and make a conscious choice to question the validity of them. Every time we have a "*what if*" thought, we can do one of two things: we can dismiss it or we can develop it into a full-fledged terror attack on ourselves. "What if the birth goes the same way as last time?" "*What if ....*"

With each negative "what if" that *we* give life to, our moods go lower and lower and our fear levels go higher and higher. But if we know that thoughts by themselves have no power and that we can question the validity of any thought that comes in our heads, then we can let thoughts go when we want to, or at least not take them so seriously.

Here's another story that happened *after* I started learning these principles. The routine blood work of one of my children showed elevated sugar levels. My pediatrician sent me immediately to an endocrinologist. It took a couple of weeks to get the appointment with the endocrinologist, and then the first thing she did was to retake the blood work, and we had to wait another few weeks for the results. It took at least a month to find out what the elevated sugar meant. The "old me" would have been thinking (worrying) the whole time: "What if she's diabetic, what does that mean? Will she ever get married and have kids," etc., etc. Our thoughts can take us anywhere if we let them. But because of my new awareness of this approach, I was able to choose to do absolutely nothing! I simply waited until we got solid results. I did not terrorize myself with all of my negative "what if" thoughts. When my child saw that I wasn't in a state of panic, she actually came over to me and asked me if I cared about her.

"What do you mean?" I asked.

She said, "You don't seem worried at all. I could have diabetes, you know. Don't you care?"

(As a side note: For a child to say this means that we have conditioned her to think that worrying about her means caring. Again, this is conditioned thinking and false, unhelpful thought.)

I asked her, "Were you diagnosed with anything yet? No, so until the blood work comes back, what will worry do? It will only make the entire household nervous and scared. If the blood work comes back all right, then we have wasted all this time being scared about nothing. What we *could* do while we are waiting is to pray that nothing is wrong. *That* would be productive."

She understood what I was saying and because I didn't play the "what if" game, the entire household was calm. I'm not saying that "what if" thoughts didn't try to sneak in;

they did, but I didn't give them any energy, so they simply passed through. You should know my daughter was not diabetic, thank G-d.

Chapter 3

Where does experience come from?

If we have a thought and attach ourselves to it, an experience is created. The first step in this is being aware that there are thoughts in your head in the first place. Once you understand that your feelings aren't coming from the circumstances or problems in your life, but from your thoughts surrounding the circumstances or problems, your life will start to look very different. As you start to question your thoughts, but more importantly your belief in those thoughts, new thoughts will float in to your mind. Being aware of which thoughts we have consciously or unconsciously attached ourselves to is where our free will is most effective. Once we are aware we are thinking something, we have an option to question that belief, and are orienting ourselves to receive different, hopefully better and more helpful ones. We can't force ourselves to let go of thought, but we can *want* new thought to come in. The principle of Mind is in charge of when that happens. When a situation comes up in our lives, we will receive different thoughts about that situation. The thought we believe to be true is the reality we will experience.

If you lose your job and believe the fearful thoughts in your head, you will feel scared, and that fear will feel very justified to you. By the same token, if you believe the optimistic thoughts in your head, then you will feel optimistic and that feeling will be very justified to you. Our experiences are created by our beliefs in our thoughts; questioning those beliefs is the start of any new experience.

Circumstances do not create our emotions; Only our attachment to thoughts does.

A human being thinks all the time, twenty-four hours a day, seven days a week. That is a physiological and psychological fact, though we may not be aware of it. Do we think about the fact that we are breathing every minute of the day? No. Intellectually we know we are breathing, but we just don't think about it. It's the same with thoughts; because we are thinking all the time, it is easy to forget that we are doing it. If we forget we are breathing, it doesn't really matter, but when we forget we are thinking, some serious problems, such as depression and unhappiness, can occur in our lives. The reason is that *our thoughts will always visit us in the form of a feeling.* Study that line well; it is the key to it all.

I was speaking to someone who needs tuition assistance from the school her kids attend. She was literally crying about how she can't do this every year. She's tired of begging the school to let her kids in at a lower rate. The whole experience, from filling out the paperwork to actually sitting in the room with the committee had her stressed and depressed. We would think she's right; anyone who has gone before the tuition assistance board knows it's not a fun experience. The question is, what makes the experience—the actual meeting or your thoughts about the meeting?

Let's analyze. My friend was anxiety-ridden from the time she received the paperwork. The paperwork is nothing; it's just forms. What gave her the anxiety were the thoughts around the paperwork. When she finally sent it in, she told me she felt relieved that one step was done. Again, paper is neutral; only her thoughts around filling out the paperwork and what that meant could cause her anxiety. If she knew that her anxiety wasn't caused by the paperwork or even the filling out of the paperwork, but instead by her thoughts surrounding the paperwork, she may have had an easier week. Why? Understanding that our experience or our feelings come from our thoughts, and that those thoughts will eventually pass through without any help from us, allows us to stop trying to fix either the circumstance or the feeling surrounding the circumstance. According to this understanding there is nothing to do. Our thoughts/feelings flow naturally without any help from us. Let's go further. Now she's anxious about the meeting, I asked her, "Did you have the meeting?"

"No."

"So, basically you are thinking about the outcome of the meeting. This means your thoughts are full of fear. What if they don't give me what I want, what if my kids don't have a school, who will accept them if this school doesn't accept them? At this point, nothing like this has happened, so the only place your feelings of fear and anxiety can come from is from your own thinking." I asked her, "Did it work out last year?"

She said, "Yes…."

"Are you able to pay the tuition that you agreed upon?"

"Yes…."

"So what are you scared of? The famous answer that plagues and terrifies all of us consists of two tiny little words: WHAT IF."

I can't tell you the amount of fear and anxiety that are encompassed by those two words. What if I can't do this or that? What if it doesn't work out this year? Worrying about "what if" isn't going to change the outcome, it's only going to put you into a state of anxiety and depression until whatever is going to happen, happens. Thoughts of "what if" are equivalent to sending yourself a threatening letter and then believing it. Does that make sense? We have to know that our mind is capable of thinking back on past events and thinking about upcoming events, almost as if they were happening at that moment, right in front of you, even though they are not. What makes matters worse is that your mind can add drama to the thoughts you're having. Your mind can replay a 5-minute argument and make it last hours, days, months, or years.

Have you ever heard of stories in which people have a fight and then don't talk for years because they are angry? Then a tragedy happens and they see each other again and are instantly friends. If you ask them what the original fight was about after they made up, the answer is almost always "I don't remember". The reason they aren't angry anymore is precisely because they don't remember; they finally stopped thinking about it. Only when we stop thinking about it can it truly end. We need to live life today, not in the past and not in the future. Live in real time as it is happening; no anticipation, no regrets. I'm not saying you shouldn't learn from past mistakes or try and prepare for future events, I'm saying once you learn from the past mistake, it's over—don't think about it again. The only place that that past mistake can hurt you is in your thoughts. You may say to me, What if I hurt someone and there are lasting repercussions? I can't simply forget about it; after all, the person is still hurt. As long as you tried to make amends and help that person in any way you can, you certainly can learn from past mistakes and move on. That is what we call repentance. If the person is still upset with you, then that person is still living in her thoughts. The opposite is also true, if someone wronged you and you can't forgive them, you are living in your thoughts. Why is it helpful to forgive ourselves, or someone else, for a bad action that was taken? Believe it or not when we forgive, we allow ourselves to *STOP THINKING ABOUT IT*. When we stop thinking about it, we stop feeling all those horrible feelings, because the feelings are coming from the thoughts in our head, not the circumstance.

Remember, we are all in the same boat here; we were all raised thinking that our thoughts were true. If this person can't forgive you, or you can't forgive her or yourself, it's because everyone still believes the thoughts in their head are true. Everytime we focus on a thought that should be dismissed, or a thought that comes with a negative emotion, that is the experience we will have. Again, it is always our belief in a thought that creates our experience of the circumstance, not the circumstance itself that creates our experience.

I know a story of twin sisters that were raped. One sister focused and believed the thoughts that told her, this event doesn't define you, you are not broken, it happened but it's over. This sister went on and had a very happy productive life. The other sister, very innocently focused on the thought in her head that said, you are ruined, you are damaged, this event has ruined your life. This sister went on to become a drug addict, with severe depression. Her life did not go very well. What happened here? Two people, same circumstance, very different outcomes. If the circumstance dictates our emotions then either both sisters should have had good lives or both sisters should have had bad lives. How could 2 people experience the same circumstance so differently? When the second sister learned about these principles, it allowed her to question the thoughts in her head. Once she did, she oriented herself to new ways to think about her experience, and herself. She listened for the thoughts that came with a feeling of truth and peace. She didn't go out looking for these thoughts, but simply trusted that they would show up. As far as I know, she is now leading a very productive life.

Moods

As human beings, we experience what we call moods. Moods are simply long-term feelings. In a low or bad mood, I experience low or negative feelings. In a high or positive mood, I experience high or positive feelings. Any feeling, high or low, comes from a thought. Sometimes though, we don't know what thought we are thinking. I remember when I first learned this, I used to tell my teacher all the time, "I am in a low mood, but I am not thinking anything." That was not true, I *was* thinking something, I just wasn't aware of the thought. Many times, the thoughts we have energized are subconscious. As human beings it is normal to experience mood swings. What we mistakenly do when we get into a low mood is to think that we need to do something to get out of it. But remember what we said earlier about that cut finger. If we just leave it alone, it will heal itself. The same thing is true of our moods. If we just leave the moods alone, which means not getting caught up in the fact that our body doesn't feel good at the moment, the mood will pass.

Think of a heart monitor. We know that a human being has a heartbeat because the lines go up and down. If the line is flat, the person has died. We are not meant to flat line, which means we are not meant to feel the same emotion twenty four hours a day. If we are alive, the mood line is moving. When we wake up in the morning in a low mood, we often feed it instead of ignoring it. As we feed it, we feel worse and worse, our mood goes lower, and our anxiety levels go higher. If we feed that low mood enough, we can put ourselves in a clinical depression, or worse. Depression is usually the result of us thinking that our low moods, which are direct results of our thoughts, define us. We think we are depressed. The truth is you are not depressed you just have depressed thoughts running through your head, and depressed feelings running through your body. When you understand that that it isn't you, it is just thoughts, you would no longer need to fix it, because all you would be fixing is energy in the form of thought. Think of it like this: You are wearing a red shirt; you look in the mirror and realize that you hate the way you look in the red shirt. What you would do then is take off the shirt and put on one you liked better. But if you thought you were the red shirt or you thought the only way to get the red shirt off would be to take your arm off with it, you would not take off the shirt. What you would probably do is just try to resolve yourself to wearing the shirt. You might try and make it look a little better but you would not take it off. Why? Because no one would *consciously* cut their arm off. What I am suggesting is this: we all think *we are our thoughts, and that our thoughts are us* when we believe that we would not let our thoughts go because we think we are letting a piece of ourselves go at the same time. The act of understanding that your thinking is just the shirt that you wear, and that the shirt is not attached to you, will allow you to change the shirt. The first step in this approach is to separate out your thoughts from you. You are not your thoughts. I guarantee you that as you start letting thought go, the person you think you are will probably not be the person you truly are.

A friend of mine sent me a client who was speaking very seriously about committing suicide, She had been in therapy for the last year and her desire to commit suicide was not only not diminishing, but getting stronger. We spoke for a while and I asked her why she wanted to commit suicide. She answered, "I can't handle the way I feel, I am angry all the time, nothing ever goes my way. Also while in those feelings of anger I lash out at people I love verbally."

"I am an angry abusive person". The first thing we spoke about was the fact that she is not an angry abusive person; she had angry abusive thoughts and those thoughts translated into angry abusive feelings that she felt in her body.

"What's the difference?" she asked.

"It is all the difference, because right now you are identifying yourself as angry and destructive. What if that is not true, what if they are [just] thoughts in your head that you believe, and that is all they are? What if they are just this ugly red shirt that you are wearing right now? The only reason you didn't change the shirt was because no one reminded you that you have the free will to take that shirt off anytime you want, and put a new one on, one that you like and look good in."

When this client saw what I was saying, her whole life changed. She started living her life again and enjoying it.

Do not trust your thinking while in a low mood

When we are in a low mood, most of the thoughts that come to mind will be low or unhelpful thoughts. Remember that the thoughts we energize and believe in in the moment are what will produce feelings that seem real to us, even if they are not. Also, in a low mood, our common sense and good judgment are off. If you are in the middle of cooking and you get a phone call telling you that your mother has been admitted to the hospital, are you more likely to touch a hot pot without putting on your oven mitts if you get nervous and scared, or if you remain calm? We all know that you are more likely to burn yourself on the pot if you get nervous and scared. There are two important points here. First, there is the fact that you have a choice to either get nervous or to remain calm; remembering that if the circumstance caused your emotions you would not have these options. Second, nervous and anxious feelings put us in a low mood that blocks our connection to our own inner wisdom and common sense. When that connection is blocked, we will make more mistakes. In low moods, we cannot easily connect to our common sense and inner wisdom. A different way of saying this is that we block our connection to our source, the formless energy behind life. That energy is the source of common sense and inner wisdom. The consequence of blocking our connection to our source is fear, anger, confusion, anxiety, depression and so on. The reason these emotions come up is that we are being directed to realize we are blocked at that point. We know because it does not feel good to be blocked from our life source. While in any of these emotional states, we should try not to act out of our ideas because they probably won't have the best outcome. Ideas we have in this low state probably do not come from our inner wisdom or common sense. If we find ourselves in any of these emotional states, the best thing to do is try to quiet our minds, and to let the thoughts pass. If we cannot drop the thoughts or they are not passing through, then we must try to ignore them, or at least not take them seriously. We should try not to act out on them. In the beginning, this seems somewhat hard. But the more deeply we understand that our negative feelings are caused by our thoughts, and that they do not define us, the more our negative low mood thinking won't bother us, and the faster those thoughts will pass, and the quicker our moods will rise.

Have you ever found yourself in the exact same situation, and noticed that you reacted differently depending on the mood you were in at that moment? One of my clients had a beautiful insight about this. She said, "It's like when the kids spill water. If I am in a good mood it really won't bother me. I will tell them calmly to clean it up. But if I am in a bad or nervous mood and the kids spill the water, watch out, I am already yelling, 'Can't you be more careful? Clean it up quick!'" She said that she never realized it wasn't the spilled water; it was her thinking about the spilled water that caused her reaction. This same client told me she is a much better mother today because she doesn't react as fast anymore when things get spilled or are little out of control in the house. To the best of her ability, she watches her moods and thinking before she reacts.

Chapter 4

Insight and Healthy Psychological Functioning
Ego and the Higher Self

We all have a place inside that is wise, calm, resilient and full of common sense. It is the place that knows that everything will be all right even in the worst circumstances. It is the part of us that can see the bright side of things, give the benefit of the doubt and rise above even the worst situations and hardest events in our lives. It is the part of us that some scientists or psychologists would call our higher self, the source of healthy psychological function. I am going to call it our soul. This is the spiritual part of us. Ideas and thoughts that come from our soul have very different feelings associated with them than the ideas and thoughts that come from our lower selves or egos.

What is an insight?

What is a thought from your soul? It is a thought that often comes with such an intense feeling of truth that many times it can be life changing. I call it an insight, which simply means a thought from the calm, wise place within. Let me give you an example. You know on an intellectual level that fire is hot. You know you shouldn't touch it because you could get burned. But until you know fire is hot from an experience or an insight, you may still touch the fire. The only way you would never touch a fire is if you have actually touched fire. Once you have touched fire you would really *know* that fire is hot. Insight is getting something at this same basic and powerful level of truth. It's the difference between knowing intellectually and deeply understanding something. Insight is to see a truth so clearly that we cannot think anything else. To have insight is to connect with our source of life and in that moment, either see something for the first time or understand something we thought we knew, but at a deeper level.

Habitual Thinking and Original Thought

Habitual thinking is made up of thoughts we already think. As long as I choose to think a thought in the same way I always have, that is all I will ever see. For example, say you know a person to be very arrogant, and you can even prove it to me. You can tell me stories that in your mind prove your point. I am suggesting that the only thing keeping your opinion in place about that person is your habitual thoughts. Every 'proof' you give me is still your thinking. When you let that thinking go, you may be able to think something else. As long as you stay in your ego and refuse to understand that you have energized certain thoughts, and because you believe those thoughts to be true, they will look and feel real to you, but in reality all they are are thoughts, nothing more, nothing less. Until you leave the possibility open that those thoughts may not be true, you will never be able to see that person in any other way. What is original thought? It is either a brand new thought, or a deeper way of seeing the same circumstance or person. Where does original thought come from? It comes from the formless energy behind life.

Anything that is formless would be limitless as well. If it is formless, it has no beginning and no end. It is formless in time as well as space. A thought is this formless energy taking a form and once it takes form it becomes limited and finite. By definition, limited and finite things wither away and die. Any thought that we think has a life span, unless we keep energizing it with our consciousness. Without the energy of consciousness, thoughts will come into our minds and flow out. In this sense they are like water. A flowing river always brings new water. But if you stop a river from flowing and let the water stagnate, it will become putrid and spoiled. Our thoughts can be the same way. The longer we hold on to a negative thought, the more unhelpful it becomes. We mistakenly think that if we let go of our thinking, nothing else will come. We hold on to what we think because we don't realize that there is any other way to think. But remember, this formless energy behind life is limitless and that means the **potential for new thought is also limitless.** The possibilities of new ways to think are endless. Our egos don't want us to believe this because then we would have to admit that we may be wrong or we don't have all the answers. It is very freeing when we can admit that we don't have all the answers, but there is something bigger than us that does. We are a part of that energy. And by the fact that we are part of that energy means that we have access to all the wisdom and common sense that it has. We are not alone, and we don't have to figure everything out by ourselves. We have something to lean on and to rely on. We just have to exercise that privilege. But first, we have to know we have the privilege.

One of my clients said that her mother always treats her worse than her siblings. "I am the Cinderella of the family," she said. When I asked her why, she said she thinks that her mother thinks she isn't as capable as the others, so she is always criticizing her. She said it is very hurtful. I asked her if there was any other way she could experience this circumstance. "You are interpreting your mother's behavior to mean she doesn't think highly of you. What if that is just a thought that you believe in this moment. What if that thought is stopping you from seeing some other possibility?" I told her to be open to the possibility that her thought may not be the only one and see if she gets any insight or original way of perceiving this situation.

She came back for her next appointment with a big smile on her face. "What happened?" I asked. She said she was talking with her mother and her mother asked her to help her with something, and then as usual started to criticize her. My client started thinking her old thoughts and started to feel her usual hurt feelings. Then she realized that it was a *thought* that was causing her to feel upset, not her mother. In that moment, she chose to ignore that thought and try to see her mother in a new way. She said the insight she got hit her like a ton of bricks. All this time she had been thinking that her mother thought less of her when she asked her to do things differently or criticized her. She said in that moment she realized that it is the exact opposite. The reason her mother is so critical of her is because she expects *more* of her than the others. She actually thinks she is *more* capable than the others. What is so interesting is that the same stories that she had used to prove to herself and to me that her mother thought less of her were the stories she used now to show that her mother thought *more* of her. It's the way we think of a circumstance that determines how we feel about it. Now when her mother criticizes her, she just laughs and actually sees it as compliment. Helpful, healthy thoughts come with a good feeling, a feeling of truth, a feeling of peace. These are the thoughts we want to energize and believe. Those are the helpful, true thoughts. Any thought that comes with a negative emotion – fear, anxiety, confusion, resentment, frustration – these are the thoughts we want to ignore and let pass, or at least question.

The Triangle Chart

Look at the triangle chart below. As you look at the section which reads, "ego, you can see how wide it is. In that section there is much room for thought. As we climb up the chart towards our "higher self," we have less and less room for thought. At the highest point of the chart, there is basically room for only one thought. As human beings we can only be aware of one thought at a time. At the bottom of the chart, where I am identified with my ego, the thoughts are coming at me fast and furious. As I climb the chart toward my higher self, my thinking

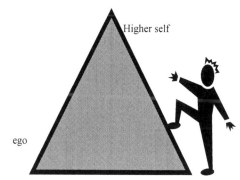

slows down until I am slowly and calmly thinking one thought at a time. The ego screams that it wants to be heard. The higher self, or the soul, doesn't scream. Why is that?

You want to decide between buying a diamond or a cubic zirconium. If a cubic zirconium salesman is going to convince you to buy the zirconium instead of the diamond, that convincing is going to take a lot of words. The diamond salesman doesn't have to say anything except, "This is a diamond." If you can afford either one, there really is no choice unless the fake-diamond dealer can convince you that there is. The ego is selling us fake goods in the guise of the real thing, therefore he really needs to speak a lot to sell them. The higher self is selling us the diamond. We don't need to be convinced that the diamond is better because it's obvious.

Here's another example of what this might look like.

I come home and the house is a mess. My kids are sitting around as if there is nothing wrong. In ego mode my thoughts could sound like this: "I can't believe these kids. Can't they ever clean up after themselves? What are they thinking; what's wrong with them?" These thoughts would come one after the other, fast and furious, and the feelings in my body would be anger and frustration. But let's say in the midst of all this, I get an insight that there are a lot of thoughts in my head, As a result of that insight my thoughts usually would lose some of their hold on me. Then I start climbing the triangle towards my higher self.

As we first get awareness that we are thinking something, we then can make a free will decision if we want to believe and act out of those thoughts or not. We will actually have a chance to take a step away from it and figure out in the moment if it is helpful thinking or not. I might ask myself, "Is this fast and furious angry thinking going to get my kids to clean up the mess, or is it just going to cause a fight?" As we become aware of our thinking we can actually evaluate or decide how to handle the situation in a way that will get better results in the moment.

But let's say that in the moment, I was not gifted with an insight, and acted from my ego; what then? Later, when I am calmer, I can reflect on what happened and hope not to get so caught up next time.

Let's say that I am gifted with an insight that I am in fast and furious thinking, but for some reason the thoughts stay in my head, and the feelings stay in my body. Let me explain through a parable. Two of my kids are playing together and one decides that he is going to bully the other by saying nasty things to him or by making fun of him. The second child comes to me and asks me to get his brother to stop. The problem is the brother won't stop. One of the things I might tell the bullied kid is to ignore his brother. I might use sentences such as, "Whatever he is saying to you is not true, so just don't pay attention." Or "If you ignore him long enough, eventually he will go away." Or maybe, "If you don't show him that it bothers you, then it won't be fun for him. The whole fun of it is annoying the other person." In fact, the ego is like that bully. It is true that while I ignore the ego, I may have an uncomfortable feeling in my body. In the case with the kids we know that the feeling is coming from the thoughts he is thinking about being bullied. I am suggesting, just like we tell our kids to ignore their sibling if the sibling is bothering them, if the ego doesn't listen to us when we tell it to be quiet, then the next thing we should do is to ignore it. If we don't take our thoughts and feelings so seriously in the moment, eventually the thoughts will go away.

You may tell me you don't like being stuck in that negative emotion. What I am suggesting here is that we change our relationship to our thoughts and emotions. Notice, I didn't say we have to change our thinking, or our emotions, I am not teaching cognitive therapy here. I said we have to change the relationship to our thinking, and emotions. That means that if in a certain moment I find myself in unhelpful thoughts or feelings like anger, depression... In that moment I would know to NOT TAKE MY THINKING SERIOUSLY. For some reason most of us think that our thoughts are true, and worse, that if we feel something we must have a reason for feeling it. I am sorry to tell you that that is completely untrue. What is true? Our feelings are our guidance system, but they are not here to guide us as to when to feel a negative emotion, they are here to tell us if we are in a negative emotion, DON'T TRUST YOURSELF IN THAT MOMENT, because any ideas that you get while in that low state of mind will only be low thoughts and bad ideas, because those thoughts come from the ego not the Higher self. Not being afraid to feel our feelings is very important, because what a lot of us do, is to suppress our feelings, and instead of letting a thought and a feeling just flow through us, we very innocently choose to spend a lot of time and energy fighting the thought from coming into our head. The problem is that it takes a lot of thought to stop one thought from flowing. Let me give you an example of what I am talking about here.

 A client came to see me, because she had a lot of fear and anxiety. The first 2 days of the intensive went very well, but on the 3rd day she came in severely depressed. So much so that all she could do was lay down on the couch and nod. She couldn't even talk. We continued talking about thoughts that day, and by the end of the session, I saw that she started to calm down. When I say calm down, I mean the mental chatter in her head started to quiet down. I asked what happened, what thoughts were in her head. She started telling me about an incident that happened the night before. Her son had asked her if he could do something. She said yes, but later on realized she should have said no. She said that was what is bothering her. The thoughts in her head looked something like, "I am so stupid. I should have known to tell him no in the first place, what was I thinking?" I asked her to try and let those thoughts go and see if there was any other way she could think about it. In that moment something clicked for her and she was gifted with a powerful insight. She looked at me with a big smile on her face and said, "I am allowed to make mistakes". She said she never realized that she didn't know that. After that insight, she was a new person, smiling, and laughing. You would never know the state she was in 2 minutes earlier. For whatever reason, she had a belief that in order to be a good mother she had to be perfect the reality is that none of us can ever be perfect. In fact, our perfection is in our imperfection, in our ability to make a mistake and use our innate resiliency to bounce back, to learn and grow from our mistakes. Our challenges in life if used correctly can push us to look to G-d, to original thought. With each new insight, we are able to see the world more clearly; we are able to see the wisdom and kindness, in ourselves, other people, and in G-d. Our emotions are here to guide us to that end. In my experience, most negative emotions are a denial of some truth. In the story we just spoke about, the woman's anger came because she knew deep down inside her that she couldn't be perfect, and was angry or scared about that fact. Once she accepted that fact, she was fine

I had a friend that was having marital issues. The consensus from her family and therapists was that her husband was mentally abusive and there was really no way to save this marriage. When she started learning about the role of thought, she realized that every time he did or said something she thought of as abusive, she would go straight to hurt and angry thinking. As long as she was focusing on and believing her negative habitual thoughts about her husband, that's all she could see. Once she realized those thoughts were probably blocking her from seeing and reacting to her husband differently, she chose to let those thoughts go, and see what other thoughts came in. She said she started focusing only on the ideas that came with a good feeling when reacting to her husband. You should know within a short while they reconciled and are happier than they ever were before. What happened here? She realized that the angry hurtful thinking was blocking out the sounds of her inner wisdom and common sense. So instead of reacting to her husband in the same way she always did, she realized that if she is feeling hurt, than the thoughts in her head where unhelpful. She made a conscious decision to question any thought that came with a negative emotion, and she oriented herself to listen for thoughts that came with a feeling of truth and peace. As she looked in the direction of helpful thinking she found that helpful ideas came into her head. Those new and helpful thoughts allowed her to get through to her husband in a way she never could before. She didn't save her marriage by positive thinking, she saved her marriage by understanding that his behavior was not making her unhappy, but the thoughts in her head about his behavior are what were making her unhappy. If she lets go of the thinking she had and lets new thinking in, she may have a different experience of him and her marriage. That is exactly what happened. She realized that he was fine, completely mentally healthy, and all that was going on, was he was taking his negative unhelpful thinking seriously and so was she. That thinking was what was causing both of their negative feelings about the other. I asked her to give me an example of something she did differently. She told me whenever he said something inappropriate to her, she would tell him that was inappropriate and ask him to please not speak to her that way again. I asked why she never said that before. She answered that she thought he should know that on his own; she didn't think she should have to tell him. One of the major insights she had about her husband, was that he really did not know that some of the things he said to her were inappropriate. She realized most of the things he said and did, he didn't do to hurt her, just truly didn't know any better. The second she started pointing out to him what he was doing, he stopped doing it. I can't tell you how many clients I have that don't confront people simply because they think the other person should know better. The truth of this whole way of thinking is an underlying fear of confrontation. It doesn't always feel comfortable to confront someone that did something wrong.

I want to give you a very simple example of what I am saying. I had a client who employed a cleaning lady, to clean her home. My client was anxiety ridden from the moment she hired this cleaning lady. The cleaning lady wasn't doing certain things the way the client wanted her to. For example, she wasn't cleaning the refrigerator properly. I asked the client to, instead of getting so upset and angry that the cleaning lady wasn't cleaning properly, why not just show her the way she would like her to clean? She said she had showed her already once and now she should know. But she doesn't know, so wouldn't it be a good idea to show her again? No she should know already. This just a simple example of how fear of confrontation can affect our lives. Anyone reading this story would think, "What's the big deal? Just tell the cleaning lady what she is doing wrong. But when you are in the situation and you believe your unhelpful thinking, it will block you from your own common sense.

Chapter 5

Goals

How do I Set and Achieve Goals?

I used to think goals were only about big things that I needed for the future, For example, I might have a goal to graduate from college, or a goal to get a job in a particular industry. It was quite a shock for me to realize that goals don't have to be big. When I was first learning about the role of thought, I was constantly asking my teacher, "Now that I'm learning this, when does my child stop crying, when do I get my husband to do this thing that I want him to do?" In other words, I wanted to know when my life would be perfect.

With each question I asked, the answer would always be

the same, "Your goal is, 'How do I get my child to stop crying?'. Simply ask yourself what steps you need to take to get there."

"I don't know; that's why I'm here! This 'role of thought' thing is supposed to give me the answers!"

"It will, but the answers are inside you; I don't know the answers. Only you do."

I really didn't like this conversation very much. I was hoping that there was some magic insight that she could tell me that would fix all my problems. What I found out was that I had work to do; I had to find my solutions, all on my own.

In the beginning, the journey seemed long and hard, but I can tell you from my own experience that this is the best road we will ever travel. As we get insights on how to solve and deal with certain issues, we are also getting to know ourselves.

Many times, the way to solve a problem is to stop energizing particular thoughts. At one of the seminars on this subject I attended, someone said, "It's very nice that I have to set a goal and get there, but how do I keep frustrated and angry thoughts out of my head while I'm figuring out how to achieve the goal?"

Here is one way to look at it. You have to go from Brooklyn to Manhattan by bus. You have a choice: the first bus is crowded and hot; there is nowhere to sit and nothing to do but be uncomfortable and miserable. Another bus is air-conditioned and has many available seats, a bus on which you will have a very pleasant ride. Your problems and goals are like that bus ride. Solving problems is a journey. How you take that journey is your choice. This is possible because *happiness depends on the state of mind and not on the circumstances*. The key is always to be aware of any habitual thoughts concerning the issue at hand. As much as possible, allow yourself to be in a happy mood, and ask yourself the question you need answered.

A friend of mine was having trouble with her eight-year-old daughter. She was acting up at home and in school. At school she always said she didn't feel well, and had to see the nurse all the time. The mother tried counseling, but the consensus from teachers and counselors was that the girl was starved for attention. The mother explained that she had six other children and that she went out of her way to give as much attention as she could to this child. She felt she was giving the girl more than enough attention. This went on from September until about March, during which time the mother was learning these principles. One day she received another phone call from the child's counselor, who repeated that the child was desperate for attention. This time, instead of feeling frustrated and upset and guilty, as she usually did, she cleared her head of all thoughts concerning this problem, got herself into as good a mood as she could and asked herself, "What am I not seeing here?" In that state of mind she saw the answer.

Two of her other kids had issues at the time; one child needed to be taken to occupational therapy twice a week, which took the mother out of the house for an hour each time. The other child had some medical issues which again took her out of the house once or twice a week to doctors, and that also lasted one or two hours each time. Almost every night of the week, the mother was not home for at least an hour after the children got home. When she finally did get home, dinner had to be made, homework checked, baths taken, and so on. So while it was true that when the mother was home, she was giving the child regular attention – homework, dinner, and a few minutes of asking how her day was – that wasn't enough because this child saw the other kids going out with Mommy and getting extra attention. The mother spoke to the child and they decided that she would take the child out for ten minutes three nights a week and they would have time alone just like the other kids did.

Within a week the child did a complete turn-around. All it took was an insight, and a little work. The insight was that in reality the child *wasn't* getting enough attention, because though the mother was at home she was busy being the mom and running the house. Then when she wasn't home, she wasn't home. The mother felt overwhelmed. She was worried about the child with the medical problems, and guilty that her eight-year-old needed something from her, but that she didn't know how to give it. All her negative thoughts caused negative feelings, and when we have negative feelings, we block our connection to our inner wisdom. If we block our connection to our inner wisdom, it is difficult to get an insight, and without insight we usually can't find solutions to our problems.

Here is a perfect example of a person who would seem justifiably overwhelmed, who had every reason to be worried about her sick child and every reason to be concerned about her eight-year-old. She was doing her absolute best to deal with a difficult set of circumstances. What else could we expect from her or her from herself? Remember the principle "There is an energy behind life running the show." Our circumstances come from G-d. As long as we live our lives in the best way possible and try to stay connected to our source of life, then we have nothing to feel guilty about. We don't need to worry if something is being handled wrongly or not in the best way; there are many messengers to help us see what needs to be fixed. The daughter was there to tell her mother that something is wrong, that in fact she *was* neglected. If the mother hadn't been so busy feeling guilty and trying to justify why she shouldn't feel guilty, she would have had her ears and eyes open to hear her daughter's problem and act accordingly. Four months of needless guilt, yet the answer was there all the time. She just couldn't hear it because her guilty thoughts where blocking the voice of her inner wisdom. The mother said that when she finally got the insight, the answer she needed, she felt like a huge weight had been lifted off her shoulders. She felt free and happy. She actually said she couldn't stop laughing at herself for wasting all that time feeling guilty about circumstances she couldn't do anything about. She had wasted her energy on her feelings of guilt instead of on solutions.

How Do I Stay in My Higher Self While I Try to Achieve My Goals?

We don't need to stay in our higher selves all the time; in fact, I don't know if that is even possible. As with the heart monitor, we are not meant to stay in the same mood all day. We do need to try and be aware of when we are in a better mood, of when we are feeling connected to our inner wisdom. It is at those times that we can best make decisions on how to achieve our goals.

A salesman incorporated these ideas into his business. His goal was to have more sales and thus make more money. He only made sales calls when he was in a good mood. When he went to meet customers, he kept his mind as quiet as possible and this allowed him to hear what the customer was saying. In order to answer the customer, he listened for his own inner wisdom to come through in the moment. He didn't give the customer all the standard sales pitches, but stayed in the moment and said what felt to be right. If he didn't feel that he was in his higher self, he simply didn't make calls because he knew that at some point during the day his mood would lift. He didn't rush the process; he simply waited.

What we often do is say that we will wait for the mood to shift, but then our ego gets in the way. Then we are apt to have thoughts that say, "Why isn't it shifting? Maybe I am doing this thing wrong." That sort of thinking keeps us in the low mood. This salesman truly trusted this approach. He *knew* that if he left his mood alone, it would shift. He said that it always did. He also said his sales shot way up.

Listening

When we talk about listening, who is it we are listening to, or what is it we are listening for? There is a different way of listening than the way you may be used to. When I say listening, *I mean we are listening for a feeling.* When we listen to someone speaking, or we listen to ourselves, we should not listen to hear something we already know, but for a new idea, or for a new way of understanding a familiar idea in a deeper, more meaningful way. When we listen for a feeling, we will hear something insightful and new along with usually receiving a good feeling. It's that feeling that we are listening for.

I'd like to suggest that often what we are doing, consciously or sub-consciously, is focusing on the thoughts in our head instead of what the speaker is saying.

Let me describe to you a few common thoughts people focus on when "listening" to others. *"Helpful listening"* is where people listen to try and be helpful. While one person is talking, the listener is constantly trying to think of things that might help the other person, For example, they may respond with, "I went through something like that a while ago, this is how I handled it".

"Judgmental thinking" consists of the listener constantly judging the circumstance or the people involved. The thoughts could look something like this. "I can't believe that person did that", or "Really that is so amazing," or "I would have handled it this way".

"Insecure thinking" When we feel insecure while listening. The thoughts could look like this, "I wonder what she is thinking of me right now, or I could never handle what she is going through." These are just a few examples of the types of thoughts people focus on when they are "listening" to others.

When we focus on these types of thoughts *we are not really listening to the other person, we are only listening to our own thinking.*

When we do that, we actually can't hear what the other person is saying.

When we are focused more on the thoughts in our head than on what the speaker is saying, we miss a lot of what the person is saying, plus we miss out on more helpful ideas that can come into our mind. These helpful ideas often come with a feeling that "resonates" with us; some people call it an a-ha moment. The content of the thoughts often consist of a new idea or seeing something more clearly, and these ideas can be unexpected and very helpful.

Remember that our feelings can be tools that help us know if the thoughts we are focusing are helpful or unhelpful. When we think we are listening but we really aren't, our feelings in the moment will let us know we are not doing what we think we are doing. We are always listening for a feeling that will tell us whether we should continue on the path we are on, or if we should stop and notice where we are. The awareness that you are not listening in the moment is all you need to refocus on the person talking. This may happen many times during a conversation; in fact, it will probably happen throughout the entire conversation. Our only job is to notice the unhelpful thoughts, let them go and continue to listen, to the best of our ability. When we are listening and present, we will have a feeling of curiosity, and/or open mindedness.

A client came in who was having difficulty with his ten year old son. He said that the boy was always yelling and defying him. The client was basically at his wit's end. When we started talking about the role of thought, and also about listening, I asked him to be aware of his thoughts the next time he was talking – arguing – with his son. He came back a week later, and he said that he had asked his son to do something that his son didn't want to do. When his son said 'no', he felt his body get angry and he realized that the thoughts in his head said, "I can't take this; can't he ever just listen?" He made a free will choice to not focus on those thoughts and a new thought came to him, which said, "Let me find out why he saying no, instead of *believing these thoughts that* he is just being difficult." From a very calm and open mind, he asked his son why he said no. The son said, "I feel like you always single me out to do things, and I don't like it." Again the client said he started to feel his body get angry and the thoughts in his head said something like, "I don't single you out. I treat all of my kids equally." And again the father noticed the thoughts in his head and made a choice to not focus on them. As a result of not listening to the thoughts pounding in his head, he actually *heard* what his son was saying. He realized, whether it was his intention or not, his son was feeling singled out in a negative way. Telling his son that his beliefs and feelings weren't true, like he used to, wasn't going to work. The father said in that moment he spoke to his son in a very different way, in a way he'd never spoken before. He calmly explained to his son until his son understood, *not until he thought his son should understand,* but until the boy really understood. He listened and was present during the whole conversation. He said he never realized how much he had only listened to what he *thought* his son was saying, not to what his son was actually saying.

When we are in a conversation with someone and we actually listen to what they are saying and not to what we *think,* they are saying, we usually get much better results.

Living in the present moment

There are a few different places in time a person can live from. One place is the past. Past living can look like this: "I can't trust myself or another person because in the past he did not follow through on something". Living in the past can also look like remembering every bad or good thing that ever happened in your life. For example every time I have a spare moment I choose to remember all the times I was embarrassed or I choose to remember a time when I was abused by someone. Or I remember that time I was really successful at something. Depending on which past memories I choose to focus on, the experience I have in the moment corresponds with how negative or positive it is. Past living can be very nice, but present life can pass me by while I am in the past. In the last story every time the father and son spoke, they both went into the past and had a conversation, based on what each one said "yesterday". When they finally started listening to today's conversation, progress was made.

Future living is when we are constantly saying if I do "A" then for sure "B" will happen. "I am not happy now but as soon as I have a certain item, whether it is money, children, a spouse, a certain house… then I will be happy". Can't you be happy now? "No I can only be happy when…" When we live in the future, again our present life will pass us by. Living out of the past or the future does not allow us to make accurate decisions, because we are not seeing what is going on NOW. We are either reliving the past and making decisions based on past emotions or living in the future and making decisions based on emotions we think we might have some day. This is not very productive.

Present living: Is when we remember the past, and make decisions based on possible outcomes but we do it from the perspective of the present moment.

I had a client whose son was suffering from depression. As we were speaking I saw that she was living in the future. She said, "My son cannot live out of this state because it will ruin his life. How can he be productive, get married get a job, if he can't function properly?" She was also living in the past. "I had a grandmother who was depressed and she did not have a happy life."

I asked her, "What does your son need now?"

"What do you mean?" she asked

"You have a future picture in your head about what will happen if your son stays like this and you have a past picture in your head about what someone else looked like that suffered from depression. But what does your son actually look like today in this moment?" As human beings we can only think one thought at a time. What this mother was very innocently doing was focusing most of her attention on "what if" thoughts, and past experience thoughts, neither of which would be helpful to the situation now.

I told her, "Everytime a memory of your grandmother pops into your head, don't get caught up in it, just let it pass through. What you are looking for is thoughts that will help allow you to help your son right now, but as long as you are focusing on thoughts that won't help the situation now, you are wasting your time."

As she started living more in the present moment, she started to react to her son based on his behavior now, not based on her grandmother's behavior, and not based on her fear of what her son may look like in the future. She started reacting to him differently, she found that she was not as afraid of his depressed moods anymore and she kind of stopped focusing on them, as she stopped focusing on them, her son also stopped focusing on them. Those moods eventually got less and less. The wisdom we need to solve any situation can only come to us in the present moment. But we have to be in the present to hear them.

Know who you are today

As children, things happen to us. We can get bullied or abused, or made fun of…. If in the moment we are getting bullied and can't deal with the emotion that we are feeling, we will bury that emotion so we can get on with our life. Our body and our intellect are here to protect us. If at 7 years old I am being abused, and the only way I can survive the attack is by burying the feelings of fear and helplessness that I have, then my mind will bury those thoughts/feelings. That act of burying those feelings will help that 7 year-old child to get through the attack. In the moment, she did what she needed to do. Here is where the problem comes in. Thoughts/feelings must flow through you, so even if in the moment you were not strong enough to feel those feelings, they won't go away. They wait for you to free them so they can flow through and leave. What happens is this: people forget or don't realize they are not 7 anymore, that they have grown over the years. They probably are old enough and strong enough to feel that emotion. When I say we live in the past I mean we still think of ourselves as that little child that got hurt, but if we wake up and see who we are today and see the same situation through 17 or 20 or 50 year-old eyes the situation would look different because we are different.

Think of it like this: At 3 years old, you jumped into the pool and almost drowned. Since then you have had swimming lessons and are a good swimmer, but for some reason you are still are afraid to jump in the pool. You will walk into the pool but you won't jump. What is happening here? You are seeing that jump from the perspective of a 3 year-old who didn't know how to swim. When that 3 year-old jumped in the pool, he almost drowned. You are no longer 3 and you can swim, and when you, the good swimmer, jump in the pool, you will not drown. Until you get to the present and see yourself as you are today, not as who you were, you will have fear of jumping into the pool. When you see your present self, you will not have fear of jumping into the pool. When things happen to us as kids, we do need those walls that we put up to get through it, but life naturally makes us stronger and teaches us how to handle different things. When we live in the moment and see ourselves as we are today, we would be able to make decisions based on our abilities today and not based on our abilities of yesterday. As I said before, this is a journey of self-awareness, which means we want to keep looking at ourselves and decide moment to moment what we can do and what our limitations are. Maybe at this moment in time you are not ready to tear down a certain wall, which is fine. You keep living, growing and getting stronger eventually you will be able to. Be real about your strengths and your limitations.

I had a client that told me that when he finally faced some of the situations that he felt used to hold him back, he laughed and said he didn't know what he was so scared about; nothing happened. I told him that when he finally realized he was not 5 years old anymore, he was able to get into the present and see that situation at 25 years old.

I am not here to say the past did not happen; it did happen. What I am here to say is that it is not happening now. It's over.

I had a client who said every time she and her brother choose to go to their parents' house for a weekend or the holidays, they always seem to have the same fights. They do love each other but they can't seem to get past certain things. I started to explain to her about living in the present, not in the past. She had a very interesting insight. She said "Every time I go home it's like I am 10 years old again. I always feel like I did when I was a kid."

I told her the next time she goes to the house notice those feelings and let them go and come back to the present moment; she said she and her brother realized they were fighting old fights. When they got back into the present moment, they realized as adults there was nothing to fight about.

Thought, Feeling, Action

Most of us are trying to get through each day, so we

concentrate mostly on what we are doing, our actions. We might make lists and try to get the things on the list done. That works very well in the day-to-day running of our lives. It is surprising to learn that, from a psychological point of view, concentrating on our actions doesn't really help us at all.

Let's say your child is misbehaving in school and you want to get him to stop. You may say to the child, "You can't behave like this; it's not acceptable and you need to stop." This may get the child to stop misbehaving for a while, but we probably have not solved the problem. This is how human beings function: a *thought* leads to a *feeling*, which might lead to an *action*.

A well-known story: A man sees another man who is searching for something on the street. He asks him what he's looking for, and if he can help. The man says he lost his ring. The other man asks, "Where is the last place you saw the ring?"

The man answers, "Across the street."

The other man asks, "If the last place you saw the ring was across the street, why are you looking over here and not over there?"

The man answers, "There is no light over there. The street light is broken; therefore I am looking over here where the street light is working, because I can see much better."

The point of this story is this: There is a lot of light on our actions; we can see *our actions* really clearly. We can see if a person acts with kindness or gets angry or misbehaves, but that is not where the answers lie. If we raise our level of consciousness a little, it might seem a little darker but we will discover the feelings behind our acts. If we raise our level of consciousness a little more, we will get to an even darker seeming place, but there is where the answer is. What was the thought behind the feeling that led to the action? "I was thinking that this person has no right to treat me that way, therefore I felt angry, and therefore I yelled at him."

Once I am gifted with an awareness of the thoughts that are in my head, I can decide if that thought comes from my ego or from my higher self. How can I tell the difference? This is where we go back to what we have been saying all along. The helpful thoughts, the thoughts from my higher self, will come with a good feeling, with a feeling of inner wisdom. The unhelpful thoughts, the thoughts from my ego, will come with a negative feeling. Once I realize that the thought I am thinking is not helping me handle the situation in the best way possible, it is within my power to stop giving energy to that thought and it will dissipate, *because a thought without the energy of consciousness has no substance and cannot last*. If you find that you can't stop believing the thought, then the best thing is *to take no action* in that moment.

Let's go back to the previous example. In the moment, if you realize you are thinking that this person has no right to treat you in this way and you feel angry, can't let go of the thought, and therefore can't stop the feeling, do not take action at that moment; do not yell at the person.

You may say, "What if the person was really out of line and really should not have spoken to me that way? Should I just let him get away with it?" I give the same answer: When you have the thought that this person should not have spoken to you this way, it can come with different feelings depending on which part of you is thinking it. If that thought comes from your higher self, it would not come with anger and you would speak to the person with appropriate words, words that may help him realize that he was out of line. If that same thought is coming with a negative emotion, then it is coming from the ego and nothing you say is likely to fix the situation.

We can think exactly same thoughts in exactly same situation. We are looking for which part of us is producing the thoughts. If it is the higher self, the thoughts come with a positive feeling, and if it's the lower self or ego, they come with a negative feeling. We should *always* listen for a feeling. It is our choice which sort of feeling we want to listen to. If we experiment with the two different feelings states, we will start noticing from which feeling state better ideas emerge. We will realize that when we act from a better feeling state, things work out better than when we act from a worse feeling state.

Peace of Mind

All of us are looking for the same thing peace of mind and happiness. We all know innately what we need to get, but our thoughts get in the way and distract us. No one does anything they truly believe would hurt them. That includes addictions or any form of inappropriate behavior. We all want the same thing. When we are dealing with a person (or ourselves) that is acting inappropriately, never focus on the action, always focus on the thought behind the action. What are you looking to get from this behavior? I had a client that had a gambling addiction.

I asked him "what feeling do you get when you gamble?"

He said "The thrill I feel when I win; there is no better feeling."

"And when you lose?"

Same answer: "There is no worse feeling."

"What if you could get the same good feeling without having to risk that you might get the bad feeling?"

He said he would not need to gamble anymore. During the

course of the intensive, the client had a very powerful insight, which came with an intense feeling of peace and security. I asked him where this feeling was as good as the thrill he got when gambling, and he said it was better. That feeling is the real diamond. The feeling he got from gambling was the fake diamond. It is a short thrill, and even within the thrill he certainly did not have peace of mind. Everyone does anything because they think they need it, but when you can look past the action and guide the person back to himself he will naturally feel those feelings as he does productive things, and those feelings will come with a true feeling of peace, because just like the gambler said, you get the thrill but also the heartbreak. When we understand that all people have inner wisdom and mental health, we will trust them to find it. We just need to point them in the direction of where to look. The gambler didn't know there was anyplace else to look. He thought that in order to get the thrill, he had to get the heartbreak. When he saw that this isn't true, he didn't need to take the risk anymore. What's happening today is everyone is looking for the ring across the street where the light is good. But the ring is really on the other side in the dark. All that is really going on is people are looking for the feeling they want from the wrong direction. When you point out that the feeling you want comes from the other direction, they will naturally go to that direction. They will realize on their own that they have been buying the fake diamond, and they will naturally start buying the real one.

CHAPTER 6

Two Realities
Spiritual and Physical

As we continue on our journey of self-awareness, I would like to speak about who we are. We are souls, spiritual beings, with a body that is the clothing of the soul. You may say, "So what? How does that help me? What in fact is the difference whether I think of myself as a body or as a soul?"

To answer this question, we have to start with a few basic ideas. The Creator, the source of all life, created each of us as a soul that was and still is completely connected to Him. How does that help me? (I refer to this energy as G-d, but you can call it whatever you like.) G-d is the ultimate source of strength; I know that because only something very strong can make hurricanes, and knock over a house with a wave of water. Only something very immense can make a sun and keep it going. G-d is also the source of all wisdom. Only something extremely wise could create the exact balance of nature that exists in the world, and create a human body that works without batteries or plugs. The heart beats and the blood flows seemingly on its own. G-d is the ultimatum in anything we can think of, whether it be mercy, compassion, or anything else. If we think of ourselves as souls, then we are connected at all times to this ultimate Source of wisdom, strength, compassion, and so on.

Because of that connection I have the ability to tap into that source. Because of that connection I am strong enough to handle any situation that comes my way. I am connected to an unlimited supply of wisdom, compassion, mercy and kindness. As a soul, I see life as it should be seen, through G-d's eyes, so to speak. I think the truth, therefore I feel the truth.

The body is the opposite of the soul. The body is very limited, while the soul, by virtue of its connection to G-d, is unlimited. The body can feel physical pain; it can die. The body is weak, it can get hurt, and it can get sick, while the soul is not victim to any of these things. When I think of myself as a body, the thoughts that I identify with are apt to be opposite to the thoughts that we would identify with as a soul, For example, low self-esteem. "I feel that I am not as good as everyone else." If I identify myself only as a body, that could be true. Others might be physically smarter than I am, stronger than I am, better looking than I am. As a body, all this could be true. But as a soul, everyone is equally connected to G-d. Because of that connection, I have the ability to be as creative as anyone else in dealing with the situations that come up in *my* life. And I have the ability to be as strong as anyone else when it comes to dealing with circumstances of *my* life. Two different children might be diagnosed, G-d forbid, with cancer. One of the mothers could be beautiful, strong, and smart, while the other mother might be not so bright, not so pretty, and frail. Those physical qualities have nothing to do with their abilities to cope with this sickness. As souls, however, both mothers are on completely equal ground; they are both souls and their abilities in this difficult situation can only come from tapping into their souls' strength, wisdom and compassion, which are innate qualities of the soul. As a body, we may have less access to these qualities. If we only identify with the body, we can fall apart. Our souls cannot fall apart. As souls we have the capacity to all be equal. What we normally think of as the less capable mother, may surpass the other one as a soul.

Letting Go of Thoughts

When we speak of letting go of or not identifying with a particular thought, or when we suggest we try to see a situation from a different perspective, we are suggesting that we figure out which 'I' is talking: the true 'I', the soul, or the body. The body normally has little to do with the true 'I', the soul.

When we listen only to the body self and believe its thoughts, we can destroy ourselves through depression, anger, jealousy, anxiety, and so on. For the body, these emotions are real. They exist because if I identify with my body that is not consciously connected to the ultimate source of life. I can feel that other people can have things that I want. Therefore, I might feel jealous. Other people might do things that I would not want them to do, and therefore I could feel angry.

But if I know that I am a soul and that there is a Creator in the world, I will acknowledge and *accept* my limitations. When I understand that I am limited, I also understand that other people are also limited. If we feel negative emotions such as fear, anger, jealousy, anxiety or stress, we should recognize that these emotions come from accepting and energizing thoughts from the body, from the ego. We now understand why this is so. Because these feelings don't exist for the soul, the soul can never feel them. Things that bother us as a body, as an ego, don't bother us as a soul. As we start letting go of the body's thoughts and desires, we slowly become free. I never understood what this meant, that true freedom is freedom from our egos, but as we start freeing ourselves from the thoughts and beliefs that come from the ego, the feeling that comes with it is freedom. It is truly amazing.

As we start to recognize who we really are and who we really are not, we will automatically begin to see life from a completely different perspective, from the perspective of the soul. As we do that, we will start to enter our inner world. The more we identify ourselves as a soul, the more the light of the soul will shine. As that happens, the more we will want it to happen, because the feeling that comes with it is a feeling of joy, wisdom, peace, and, best of all, true freedom.

Chapter 7

Conclusion
We are All Equal

In conclusion, I would like to leave you with this thought. At our most basic level, human beings experience life the same way. How that manifests itself and how it takes form is what makes each of us unique. More simply, imagine that everyone has a blank canvas. On that level, everyone starts out the same. What makes us unique is what we paint on the canvas, our pictures. We are each a blank canvas and we all have the ability to paint any picture we want, and *can repaint the picture as many times as we want*. The pictures we paint will be our experience of reality. What people usually don't realize is that they are not stuck with their pictures; they can rip up their pictures and start over anytime they like. How do we draw? Our thoughts are our paints, and our consciousness applied to those thoughts becomes our perception and experience of reality. The reason any person has ever committed a crime, or has had any kind of addiction, or has been depressed or angry, is because they didn't realize they had drawn a picture of a reality and then thought they were stuck with it. The moment they realize that they are not stuck with what they think is the moment they can start again and redraw their lives.

Innate health is taught in many of the jails around the country. One of the teachers told about an insight that one of the inmates had. This story concerned a boy that had been incarcerated many times for stealing. After he listened in on a few classes, he came into one of the sessions with a big smile on his face. When the teacher asked him what he was so happy about, the boy said he just realized that if he never commits another crime he will never have to come back to jail. The teacher asked, "You didn't know that? Why did you think you were in jail?" The boy said he always thought that he was in jail because his mother was on drugs, because he was a black kid from the streets. He was always told that because of his life circumstances he didn't really have a choice but to commit crimes and be in jail. His insight was that this was not true. He was only in jail because he committed crimes, and he could choose not to commit crimes. The teacher said as far as she knows, he has never been back to jail.

We can never know why a person does anything. If you had told me that a person didn't know he was in jail because he committed crimes, I would not have believed it. But in this example, that is exactly what happened. I am not saying that criminals should not be in jail. What I am saying is that the reason we do anything is because of what we are thinking, and *that is the only reason*. We need to keep coming back to the fact that *we are the thinker*, and the thoughts that we energize and attach ourselves to are creating our perceptions of reality in the moment. The more deeply we understand this, and the more we realize that it is true for every single person on the planet, the more we won't take things so personally, or judge other people so harshly. After all, I do some really stupid things when I get into unhelpful thinking, so why it so difficult for me to understand that others can also get caught up in their thinking and do stupid things as well? When we realize we are all in the same boat, we will not waste our time trying to figure out why other people do things, or why we do things. We all act in certain ways because we are thinking certain thoughts. I don't care why you think it, I don't care if you think it because you were abused or hurt as a child, or what the reason was. The bottom line is that we need to stop energizing and accepting this type of thinking. Or better, we need to stop believing that those thoughts are true. Let them go, and your life will change for the better.

You don't need to bring up every bad thing that ever

happened to you, to try to give yourself excuses as to why you behave the way you do. You just have to take responsibility for the fact that right now, these are your thoughts. It is up to you to want let them go. When you do this, miracles will happen. Stay calm in your low moods and your high moods. Keep looking to identify the thoughts that come from your soul, your higher self, but most of all enjoy the journey. The journey is life itself.

35817017R00052

Made in the USA
Middletown, DE
15 October 2016